This Book Belongs To:

____

Advice and Special Messages

For Baby and Parents

Advice and Special Messages

For Baby and Parents

Advice and Special Messages

For Baby and Parents

Advice and Special Messages

For Baby and Parents

Advice and Special Messages

For Baby and Parents

Advice and Special Messages

For Baby and Parents

Advice and Special Messages

For Baby and Parents

Advice and Special Messages

For Baby and Parents

Advice and Special Messages

For Baby and Parents

Advice and Special Messages

For Baby and Parents

Advice and Special Messages

For Baby and Parents

Advice and Special Messages

For Baby and Parents

Advice and Special Messages

For Baby and Parents

Advice and Special Messages

For Baby and Parents

Advice and Special Messages

For Baby and Parents

1

Advice and Special Messages

For Baby and Parents

Advice and Special Messages

For Baby and Parents

Advice and Special Messages

For Baby and Parents

Advice and Special Messages

For Baby and Parents

Advice and Special Messages

For Baby and Parents

Advice and Special Messages

For Baby and Parents

Advice and Special Messages

For Baby and Parents

Advice and Special Messages

For Baby and Parents

Advice and Special Messages

For Baby and Parents

Advice and Special Messages

For Baby and Parents

Advice and Special Messages

For Baby and Parents

Advice and Special Messages

For Baby and Parents

Advice and Special Messages

For Baby and Parents

Advice and Special Messages

For Baby and Parents

Advice and Special Messages

For Baby and Parents

Advice and Special Messages

For Baby and Parents

Advice and Special Messages

For Baby and Parents

Advice and Special Messages

For Baby and Parents

Advice and Special Messages

For Baby and Parents

Advice and Special Messages

For Baby and Parents

Advice and Special Messages

For Baby and Parents

Advice and Special Messages

For Baby and Parents

Advice and Special Messages

For Baby and Parents

Advice and Special Messages

For Baby and Parents

Advice and Special Messages

For Baby and Parents

Advice and Special Messages

For Baby and Parents

Advice and Special Messages

For Baby and Parents

Advice and Special Messages

For Baby and Parents

Advice and Special Messages

For Baby and Parents

Advice and Special Messages

For Baby and Parents

Advice and Special Messages

For Baby and Parents

Advice and Special Messages

For Baby and Parents

Advice and Special Messages

For Baby and Parents

Advice and Special Messages

For Baby and Parents

Advice and Special Messages

For Baby and Parents

Advice and Special Messages

For Baby and Parents

Advice and Special Messages

For Baby and Parents

Advice and Special Messages

For Baby and Parents

Advice and Special Messages

For Baby and Parents

Advice and Special Messages

For Baby and Parents

Advice and Special Messages

For Baby and Parents

Advice and Special Messages

For Baby and Parents

Advice and Special Messages

For Baby and Parents

Advice and Special Messages

For Baby and Parents

Advice and Special Messages

For Baby and Parents

Advice and Special Messages

For Baby and Parents

Advice and Special Messages

For Baby and Parents

Advice and Special Messages

For Baby and Parents

Advice and Special Messages

For Baby and Parents

Advice and Special Messages

For Baby and Parents

Advice and Special Messages

For Baby and Parents

Advice and Special Messages

For Baby and Parents

Advice and Special Messages

For Baby and Parents

1

Advice and Special Messages

For Baby and Parents

Advice and Special Messages

For Baby and Parents

Advice and Special Messages

For Baby and Parents

Advice and Special Messages

For Baby and Parents

Advice and Special Messages

For Baby and Parents

Advice and Special Messages

For Baby and Parents

Advice and Special Messages

For Baby and Parents

Advice and Special Messages

For Baby and Parents

Advice and Special Messages

For Baby and Parents

Advice and Special Messages

For Baby and Parents

Advice and Special Messages

For Baby and Parents

Advice and Special Messages

For Baby and Parents

Advice and Special Messages

For Baby and Parents

Advice and Special Messages

For Baby and Parents

Advice and Special Messages

For Baby and Parents

Advice and Special Messages

For Baby and Parents

Advice and Special Messages

For Baby and Parents

Advice and Special Messages

For Baby and Parents

Advice and Special Messages

For Baby and Parents

Advice and Special Messages

For Baby and Parents

Advice and Special Messages

For Baby and Parents

Advice and Special Messages

For Baby and Parents

Advice and Special Messages

For Baby and Parents

Advice and Special Messages

For Baby and Parents

Advice and Special Messages

For Baby and Parents

Advice and Special Messages

For Baby and Parents

Advice and Special Messages

For Baby and Parents

Advice and Special Messages

For Baby and Parents

Advice and Special Messages

For Baby and Parents

Advice and Special Messages

For Baby and Parents

Gift Log

Name	Gift Brought

Gift Log

Name	Gift Brought

Gift Log

Name	Gift Brought

Gift Log

Name	Gift Brought

Gift Log

Name	Gift Brought

Gift Log

Name	Gift Brought
1	

Gift Log

Name	Gift Brought

Gift Log

Name	Gift Brought

Gift Log

Name	Gift Brought

Gift Log

Name	Gift Brought

Gift Log

Name	Gift Brought

Made in the USA
Columbia, SC
24 October 2024

44954430R00067